Mail Merge Explained

All About Lists

Dr. Timothy Haupt, Psy.D

10/10/2011

By: Dr. Timothy Haupt, Psy.D.
Copyright Application: 1-672882241
For: Students everywhere
First Edition

❡ TABLE OF CONTENTS ❡

APPENDIX A – STORING DOCUMENTS...............54

APPENDIX B – THE OUTPUT DOCUMENTS.......57

Some of the product names, web sites and company names included in this booklet have been used for identification purposes only and may be trademarks or registered trade names of their respective manufacturers and sellers. The authors, editors and publisher disclaim any affiliation, association or connection with, or sponsorship or endorsements by, such owners.

ISBN: 978-1466459311: 146645931X

Please Note: If you find errors on this booklet, please send corrections to drtlhaupthhh@gmail.com . You will earn brownie points for your efforts and maybe a cookie.

Printed in the United States of America

Copyright Information

All about Lists

Mail Merge is all about lists. If you have a letter to send, usually you have a list of people you wish to send that letter to. Whether you send Christmas Cards or business letters, print "Hello" labels or business cards, it's about the lists. If not for lists, your work could not be sent anywhere.

Mail Merge is taking a single letter (Template) and sending it to multiple recipients on a list (Data Source).

This booklet is designed to help you get up and running with your list as soon as possible. If you follow along carefully and practice, you will begin to become familiar with the mail merge process.

Assumptions

- This booklet assumes you have a basic understanding of Word Processing and Spreadsheets. If you are not familiar with either concept, you should study up before completing the work in this booklet. Try using the free tutorials on http://www.microsoft.com/

- This booklet also assumes that you know how to save a document and create folders. If you do not understand these concepts, there are many resources on the Internet that are designed for you to get up to speed in those areas. http://www.jegsworks.com/ is one of those places.

What this book is:

This book is designed to help you with Mail Merge on PC Compatible Computers.   While there are advanced functions available, this booklet focuses in on the basic process associated with merging letters with lists.

What this book is NOT:

This book is not designed for those who do not have a basic understanding of how to use computers and software. If you do not understand what files or folders are, you need to do further study as mentioned above.

A Little History

Enter the Typewriters – Better than Printing Presses

Around 1867[1], the typewriter was invented and life got easier. Typing freed many companies from the printing press – which probably made a lot of typesetters angry.   Since that time, typing has been an integral part of government and business process. Imagine typing out forms all the time to people. Sending out the same form to many people required individual typing of the address – at the very least. Sometimes, we would miss a whole page of people on our list!! And often, no one would notice.

Form Letters

Sending the same letter or "*form letter*" to a lot of different recipients used to be a royal pain.   In the days of Royal typewriters, the same letter had to be typed over and over again with a different addressee at the top.   (For more information about addressees please look up "*Block Letter Format*" on the Internet, or the OWL at Purdue™) A technological breakthrough known as carbon paper allowed the typist to create duplicates of the same letter while only typing it once.   In 1954, carbon paper was outdated with the use of "No Carbon Required" (NCR) paper.

By 1983, carbon paper was almost a thing of the past. NCR paper was a breakthrough that allowed the typing of many multiple copies of the same document.   Unfortunately, the addressee could not be altered unless you had buckets of whiteout at your disposal[1].

Back in the olden days (before Mail Merge), documents had to be repeatedly typed manually on an IBM Selectric™, invented in 1961[2].   If copies were required, we had to use carbon paper or carbonless paper.

Enter the Word Processor.

In 1964[2], the first word processor was introduced by IBM.   A Breakthrough indeed! Imagine not having to type each letter individually, but typing the same thing once and printing it over and over.   However, the addresses did have to be typed over and over using a single strip typewriter.

Enter Mail Merge 1.0

On some of the older programs, the names, addresses, cites, etc were stored with the original document.   This, however, caused quite a few problems – especially when the main document was erased.   When that happened, the address list was erased as well. Erasing a master document without the trusty "Are you sure?" prompt caused a lot of headaches and time consuming work.

Enter Mail Merge 2.0

More modern techniques allow the storage of the main letter and the address lists to be stored separately. MS Word 2007 has a variety of options at your fingertips to make your mail merge life much easier.

Mail merge is taking a letter template (**Master Merge Document**) and merging it with an address list (**Data Source**). The result is an **Output Document** that you will actually print out and send to your recipient list.

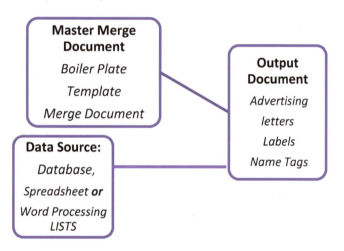

Fig 1 Illustrating the Merging of Word with Access, Word or Excel

There MUST be three documents if you will be mail merging.

1. The **Master Merge Document** has all the information you want to send to an address list. It can be a memo, a letter, a set of labels, a schedule, or pretty much anything you want to send to a lot of people. You do not generally print this document out unless you need to for documentation purposes. This can be called a "*template*", "*boilerplate*" or "*merge document*" in the workplace.

2. The **Data Source** has the names, addresses, etc of the people you will be sending the letter to. The Data Source can be an Access Database, an Excel Spreadsheet or a Word Document. This can be a customer list, address list, customer database or whatever. This database is relatively stable usually with customer names being added or taken away periodically. It can be called "the *address list*", the "*database*" or "*merge source*" in the workplace. It doesn't have to be an access database. It can be a spreadsheet or a MS Word document.

3. The **Output Document** is the actual letter(s) that you print and send to the recipients on your address list. It is not always saved as it is usually changed periodically (monthly, weekly, daily) as information changes and updates are sent out.

Mail merge has a variety of uses.

- Internal memos that update department heads on the important numbers of the month.
- Schedules to be sent to volunteers for non-profit agencies.
- Mailing Labels for use of Form Letter Mailings
- Name Tag Stickers for meetings
- Agency reports to external auditing companies
- Sales letters to selected customers in specific areas of the country
- Informational updates to stockholders
- Grade reports to students that are linked to your Excel spreadsheet.
- Anything that has a lot of Lists, Lists and more Lists

Creating the Merge Documents

From the Beginning

Before we can send a merged list, we need to make some choices. First, what are we going to send?

In this case, you are seeking employment and you need to send a letter outlining your talents to a list of employers.

As stated earlier, we MUST have a **Master Merge Document** as this is what we will be merging with the list we create.

Creating the Master Merge Document

The **Master Merge Document** is a "boilerplate". A boilerplate is used over and over again. Within this document, you insert merge fields that will access a **Data Source** (to be explained later). All the editing functions must be done in this document; otherwise, you will have tens or hundreds of corrections to make. **NEVER** make corrections in the merge **Output Document** (explained later).

In order to create your
Master Merge Document
you must open MS Word 2007.

Save the document as *Master Merge Document 1*

If you do not know how to open MS Word
ask your instructor or a friend for assistance

Fig 2 MS Office Word Selection in Windows XP

You have now created your **Master Merge Document**, but it has no content.

In order for us to have content, type the letter as shown on Figure 3. Type the bolded areas exactly as shown as they will be replaced with Field Codes. Field codes are also known as MERGE FIELDS.

Merge Fields are the *Address, City, State, Zip Code, First Name, Last Name, Employee Number, etc.* These elements or *Field Names* are what change in your **Master Merge Document.** If you want to learn more about Field Names, go to http://word.tips.net/ .

Please key the bold areas in exactly as shown in Figure 3 as it will be used when we "put it all together" at the end of this chapter. Remember to save it as **Master Merge document 1**

 TIP 1: *Word automatically includes the .doc or docx at the end of your document name so you do not have to enter it.*

Date

Address

Greeting

Salutation:

I am interested in the position of administrative secretary with your company.

I have ten years experience as an executive secretary with Fluor Corporation in Irvine, California. In that position, I coordinated schedules, paying of corporate accounts, billing customers for hours and acting as liaison to the Chief Financial Officer. In my duties, I was the "go to" person for issues that revolved around company scheduling of trainings and seminars.   I was very efficient, timely and you can phone my boss at 714-555-1212 for more details.

I look forward to speaking with you soon.

Sincerely

Jane Q Public

Fig 3: Letter of Interest Template

The **bold** items you entered cannot have merge fields entered yet because you must first start the mail merge process.

Fields and Records

Before we can go further, we need to talk about fields and records.   Please refer to the table below:

Every Column is a Field

Every Row is a Record	Field 1	Field 2	Field 3	Field 4	Field 5	Field 6
	First Name	Last Name	Address	City	State	ZIP
1	John	Jones	12345 Every St	Fresno	CA	93706
2	Jane	Mayville	223 Some St	Fresno	CA	93706
3	Fred	Anyhow	112 My Street	Fresno	CA	93706

Table 1: Fields and Records

The table above is a very short mailing list with false addresses. Notice the column that says "*Every Row is a Record*".   Each complete listing (**row**) is called a "**Record**".   A **Record** is a row of information.

Notice the column headings (First Name, Last Name, etc).   Each of these entries(**columns**) is a "**Field**".   A field is a single part of the whole "**Record**".   A **Field** is a column of information.

The following is a **Record**: *John Jones, 12345 Every St, Fresno, CA 93706*

A **Record** :   a record holds all the information about one item or subject. It is like one index card in an index card file[5].

A **Field:** a single slice of information from a **Record**.   For example, **John** is a field.   **93706** is a field.   These fields can be individually placed within a document as part of the mail merge process.   *Remember the bold areas you put on your interest letter?   Those will become fields.*

Remember.   Every Row is a **Record** and Every Column is a **Field**.

Test your comprehension 1

Please refer to Table 1: Fields and Records.

1. How many fields are there in each record?

   _____

2. What is the content of Field 3 in Record 2?

   _____

3. Please write record 3 completely:

   _____

4. What is in each "City" Record?

   _____

5. What is in Field 2, Record 3?

   _____

6. True or false.   A record is a single slice of information from a field. _____

7. Is **93706** a field (y/n)? _____ Why?

   _____

8. What is the content of field 4 in record 1?

   _____

What is a Row? _____

What is a Column? _____

Creating the Data Source

A **Data Source** is a list. The list can be very complicated or very simple. Do you have a rolodex? You have a data source. The phone contacts you have? That's a data source. How about your email contacts? That's another data source.

Your data source can be an **Access**® Database, an **Excel**® Spreadsheet, or a **Word**® Document. A data source is something you will use to create your mail merged Output Document.

You will not be using **Access** to create your **Data Source**. You will need to open your **Master Merge Document 1** that you created earlier. Open that file. After you open the file, select the Mailings Tab on the Ribbon (Fig 4).

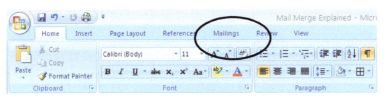

Fig 4 – The Microsoft Ribbon - 2007

 TIP 2: Mail merge is a left to right process. Moving from the left, you have to **Start Mail Merge**. Next, you have to **Select Recipients**. And so on. Remember to move left to right when starting a mail merge.

Fig 5 – Mailings Tab

Start Mail Merge

As you look at the Mail Merge Tab part of the MS Ribbon, you notice that almost all of the ribbon is grayed out. You must first decide what kind of mail merge you will be using before you can use the features in the "Mailings" tab. You can either select the Envelopes or Labels button. Since we already have a letter that we typed (**Master Merge Document 1**), we do not need to select "Start Mail Merge" this time.

Select Recipients

Mail merge is using a list of names and addresses (Recipients) over and over on the same letter, or boiler plate (**Master Merge Document**). Before we can begin to create our mail merge, we must have recipients ready to place in our **Master Merge Document 1**

Fig 6 – Select recipients

It is important to note that the very first step after you have decided upon which type of document to use is to select your list. "Select Recipients" gives you three options.   You can type a new list (we will do this), use an existing list and you may select from your Outlook Contacts.

Caution: Unless you have Outlook set up as a mail client, you should **NOT** use Outlook Contacts as an option.

Use the "*Type New List*" option for this exercise. We will be entering names and addresses so we can use this as our Data Source.   When you select "*Type new list*", you will see a data entry screen.   It is pre-loaded with Fields (Name, Address, etc) that will allow you to immediately enter data.

Data Entry

Enter the Title, First Name, Company Name, Address Line 1, etc.

This list will be linked with your **Master Merge Document 1**

These two files MUST be linked together in order for you to create your **Output Document**

Fig 7 – Data Entry Screen

Every Column is a Field

Every Row is a Record	Field 1	Field 2	Field 3	Field 4	Field 5	Field 6
	First Name	Last Name	Address	City	State	ZIP
1	John	Jones	12345 Every St	Fresno	CA	93706
2	Jane	Mayville	223 Some St	Fresno	CA	93706
3	Fred	Anyhow	112 My Street	Fresno	CA	93706

Table 2 - Address List

Enter the data on this list into your database. Enter Records 1, 2 and 3 into your data entry screen. If the first name is male, enter Mr. for the title. If the first name is female, enter Ms. for the title. If you have questions on how to enter data, ask your instructor or a colleague.

Name the Data List

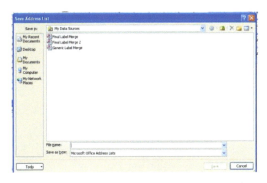

Fig 9 – Choose a Location For Your File

After you entered the records and pressed the "OK" button, it asked you if you wanted to save the document.   Yes *you do want to save it. Now,* You must choose a location for your data source.

Choose a directory

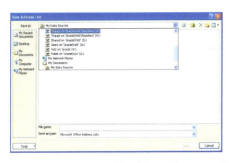

Select a suitable location for your data file. At home, you might want to select (C:\)

After you have chosen the location, you need to name your **Data Source**.

Fig 10 – Choose directory location

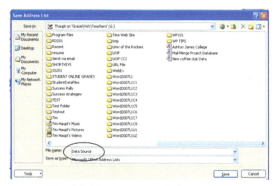

Fig 11 Name your data source

In the space circled, type **Data Source 1** Then hit the "OK" button. You now have a list!!

Wait!   After you have saved your **Data Source** file, you MUST now save your Word Document, **Master Merge Document 1**.   If you do not save your document right now, your link to the **Data Source** will not be there the next time you open the file.

Test your comprehension 2

1. The document that you will use over and over again is the boiler plate, or the _____ Document

2. The file that has all your list information (fields and records) is your _____

3. The individual items that you will merge into your main document are known as _____

4. A complete group of fields that hold all the information about one item or subject is a
_____

5. When you "**Select Recipients**", what are you preparing to create? _____

6. What two files (documents) must you have before you can start mail merge?

   a. _____

   b. _____

7. What is the actual letter that you print and send to the recipients on your address list?
_____

8. We cannot mail merge without the
_____ or the
_____

Putting it All Together

Selecting the Data Source

You have hopefully created **Master Merge Document 1** and **Data Source 1** because we will be merging them together to create an **Output Document**.   Please refer to Figure 1 in the first part of this booklet for an illustration of the process.

If you saved your **Master Merge Document** appropriately, your **Data Source** is linked to your merge document.   The way to tell if your **Master Merge Document** has a **Data Source** linked to it is to click the "*Mailings*" tab and select the "*Edit Recipients List*" button in the "Start Mail Merge" group.

If you clicked on the "*Edit Recipients*" button, you should see this dialog box (Figure 12) floating above your Word Document.

Note: If you do not see the "*Edit Recipients*" button as clickable, you need to go one button to the left and "*Select Recipients*". Find the file that you named "**Data Source 1**"   After you have Selected Recipients, save the **Master Merge Document 1**.

If you clicked on the "*Edit Recipients*" button, you should see this dialog box floating above your Word Document.

Fig 12 – Recipients Linked to Master Merge Document 1

Wait! You should have **Master Merge Document 1** linked **to Data Source 1**. If you are not sure that you have done this, please check with your instructor or a colleague. This is **critical** as you need these two documents to be linked so you can insert merge fields.

Inserting Merge Fields

TIP 3: Remember when the subject of *Fields* and *Records* came up? Now is the time to either remember or study what the two things mean before you move forward in this part of the booklet.

We will be inserting fields from the **Data Source 1** file that you have linked to the **Master Merge Document 1** file. Inserting fields is like inserting blank fill-in spots that will be completed later.

Insert the Date

- Select your first bold field – **Date**
- After you have highlighted the word Date, select the *Insert Tab* on the ribbon.
- Select the "Date and Time" from the text group

TIP 4: Make sure you check the little box that says "Update Automatically" as this will have the current date every time you open the document.

Select the first current date option.

Click "OK"

The current date should have replaced the word **Date**.

Fig 13 – Select the Date

Insert the Address Block

An address block is on the right

Fluor Corporation
Human Resources
3 Polaris Way
Aliso Viejo, CA 92698

Fig 14 Address Block

In every business letter, whether block format, semi block format or modified block format, there is an address block. Without the address block, we would not know where to send the letter. The address block is in the business letter and on the business envelope.

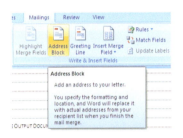

You will notice, when you select the *Mailings Tab*, that there is an individual selection for inserting the Address Block.

The address block includes company name, individual name, address, city, state and zip code.

Fig 15 Select Address Block

Select the *Mailings* Tab on the MS Word Ribbon.

Select the *Address Block* button.

You should see a dialog similar to the one in Figure 16. For this exercise, just select the "OK" button.

Fig 16 Insert Address Block

Open your **Master Merge Document 1** and highlight the word "**Address**".

After you have inserted your Address Block, you might see something like this

«**AddressBlock**»**Address**

Fig 17 Address block illustration

If you see the extra word **Address**, delete it and just leave the merge field. The Address block should look like this:

«**AddressBlock**»|

Insert Greeting Line

A greeting line is the salutation of the letter. In the days of Greeks and Romans, the greeting was "Grace and Peace to You". These days, it can be anything from *Dear John* to the ever popular *To Whom it May Concern.* If you are still on the mailings tab, you should notice the "*Greeting Line"* button. Back space over the **Greeting** entry in your **Master Merge Document 1** and insert a greeting line.

On the *Insert greeting line* dialog, select the first one that says "Dear Mr. Jones" – as shown in figure 18

Click OK

Fig 18 Insert Greeting Line

10/14/2011

You should have
these three fields in your document.   «AddressBlock»
Remember that the **DATE** is a field.

                                                                «GreetingLine»:

Fig 19 – The Date, Address Block and Greeting Line

You have now created a **Master Merge Document** that is linked
to your **Data Source**.   Remember that they are LINKED but
Separate.

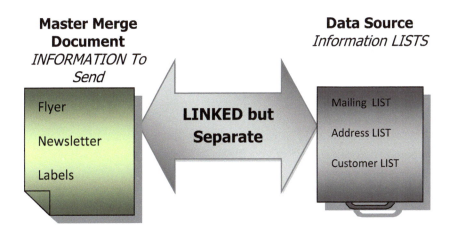

Fig 20 Linked but Separate

File Considerations

It is important that you remember that you are merging two wholly separate files.   Your **Master Merge Document** is a Word file that has the information you want delivered.

Your **Data Source** is an Access database file that has the list of people you want the information delivered to.

The **Master Merge Document** and the **Data Source** are two files that you should store in the *same directory*.   That way, when you need them, you will find them.

The final document is a *temporary* one as it is re-created on a periodic basis (daily, weekly, monthly, etc.).

 It is usually a good idea to name them similarly as you will have an easier time knowing which **Data Source** goes with which **Master Merge Document**.   (See Appendix A for more details)

Creating the Output Document

You are ready to try a Finish & Merge.   In this step of the process, you will be creating a brand new document.   The new document is what you will be sending to the people on your list. Whether you send a newsletter, print labels, or whatever, the finished product is achieved by the "Finish & Merge" button.

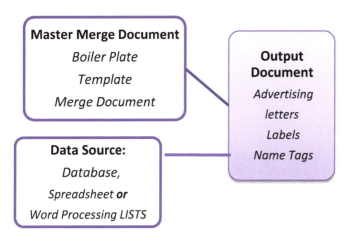

Fig 21 Creation of the Output Document

Remember that when we create the merged letters, *IT IS A SEPARATE DOCUMENT.* Depending upon what you create will determine how Word will name the file. If you create a letter, it will create a file called **Letters1**. If you create a set of labels, it will create a file called **Labels1**.

 You should be able to access the last button on the right
Finish & Merge.
For this exercise, select "*Edit Individual Documents*"

Fig 22 Finish & Merge

In the Finish & Merge, you have the option of selecting all the documents for individual editing, or just the current record (Wherever you point is where it goes), or you may select a range of records. Sometimes you only want to send your output to a smaller range of list members than you have on file. For the purposes of this exercise, *select all.*

 In the "*Merge to New Document*" dialog box, select "*All*" and then Select OK

Fig 23 – Select All

Fig 24 – Notice the Title of the document: **Letters1**

Depending upon the requirements of the office you work for, you may or may not have to save this "Letters1" document.   Keep in mind that MS Word is just giving the document a generic name. It is up to you to give it a name that has meaning.   In this case, it is the **Output Document**. Please see <u>Appendix B</u> for an example of the **Output Document.** Save it as **Output Document.**

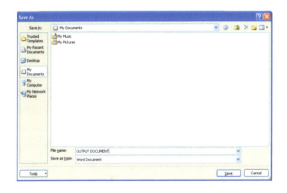

Fig 25 – Saving the Output Document

Your particular company may not require you to save this document as all they would be interested in is the finished product (Report, Customer Letter, etc.) that is produced periodically (weekly, monthly, yearly).

Things to Remember

Mail Merge is a Left to Right process

1. Choose your document (Label, Letter, Business Card, etc)
2. Start Mail Merge
3. Select Recipients (Data Base, Spreadsheet or Word Document)
4. Insert Merge Fields (Address Block, Last Name, etc)
5. Finish and Merge

Fig 26 – From Left to Right

There are THREE documents

1. **Master Merge Document** – This is the document that you save and change periodically for use in a Mail Merge. It is also known as a "boilerplate". **Always** edit your Master Merge Document.
2. **Source Document** – This is the list you want to send the content of your **Master Merge Document** to. (Database, Spreadsheet, Word Document)
3. **Output Document** – This is what you print out and send to the people on your list. **NEVER** edit your Output Document unless absolutely necessary
4. *Remember that you do not always have to save this document.* If you do, be sure to properly label this document by writer, department, content and date. (Example: ***Jones_AR_End_Of_October_2009_Report_10_20_2011***)

You are not required to use Access

Mail Merge can be used with Excel and MS Word as data sources. If you only have MS Word and MS Excel, you can mail merge.

Mail Merge is All about Lists

Mail Merge is generally used when you want to send a single letter to a lot of people on a list. You can work for a Non-Profit, Real Estate Agent or any company that uses lists.

Taking it a Bit Further

Exercising your right to know more

Exercise 1 - Merging with Excel and using "RULES"

In this exercise, you will be introduced to how you can merge your Word document with Excel.   If you have MS Office student edition, you should at least have a copy of MS Excel.   Also, if you have Open Office spreadsheet, you should also be able to use the spreadsheet to merge.

With many businesses, sales are regional.   There are sales representatives who periodically visit their regions in specific cities to perform customer service and look for new sales leads. Microsoft Word has a feature that allows you to change information on your merge document based upon the region to which you are sending the document.

Step 1: Create your spreadsheet.   Use the data below as this will be used more than once. Be sure to name it something that you can remember.

Be sure to save your file in a place you will remember (See: Appendix A)

First Name	Last Name	Address	City	State	Zip	Region	Account Number
John	Jones	1234 Best St	Clovis	CA	93612	Western	X3456
Fred	Flintstone	112 Beatdown Lane	Huntington Beach	CA	92646	Western	Y3345
Arie	Onassis	123 Heartbreak	New York	NY	10019	Eastern	X4442
Jackie	Canady	223 Midrange Dr	Oklahoma	OK	72189	Central	Y3939
Richie	Rich	339 Minlspring Rd	Ft. Lauderdale	FL	32848	Southern	X7575
Miley	Sirius	334 E. Monkey	Memphis	TN	42838	Southern	Ix399

Fig 27 Spreadsheet Data Entry – Merging with Excel

Step 2: Save your data after you have entered it exactly as shown above in Figure 27.

 TIP 5: You should enter the data with the column headings as shown because it will make your life much easier when it comes to merging.

Step 3: Open a New Word document and save it as Master Mail Merge 2. Type the letter exactly as shown in ***Appendix B, Sample Letter 2.***

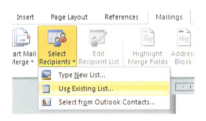

Step 4a: Select your recipients. This time, use the Excel spreadsheet you created as a data source.

Fig 28 Use Existing List

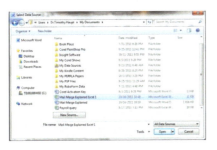

Step 4b: Locate your excel spreadsheet that you recently saved.

Select the "**OPEN**" Button.

Fig 29 Select Excel as your data source

Step 5: Refer to figure 19 on page 33 and insert the **Date**, **Address Block** and **Salutation** as shown in figure 19.

TIP 6: MS Word 2007 and 2010 inserts space after every paragraph.   This can cause problems.   Select your Address Block and salutation. Select the Home Tab and the little access button on the paragraph group. Set the "before" and "after" spacing to zero. This will eliminate any future spacing issues in your documents.

Step 6: Preview your document using the Group shown in Figure 30: Preview. You will notice the arrows that allow you to scroll through your recipients much like a photo viewer. Edit your Master Merge Document 2 until it looks suitable for printing.

This is your preview results group in the Mailings Tab. After you have linked a database to your Master Merge Document, you should be able to press the "Preview Results" button and scroll through the people on your list. TRY IT!!

Fig 30: Preview Results

Your Address and Greeting Lines should appear similar to the image in **Figure 31.**

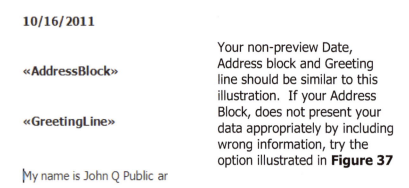

10/16/2011

«AddressBlock»

«GreetingLine»

My name is John Q Public ar

Your non-preview Date, Address block and Greeting line should be similar to this illustration. If your Address Block, does not present your data appropriately by including wrong information, try the option illustrated in **Figure 37**

Fig 31 – Date, Address and greeting line

Almost Done!

You are almost done.   However, we need to insert a date that is dependent upon the region to which you are sending your letter.

In the body of your letter, you should have a statement in bold that says **Insert Itinerary Date**.   This is a date (listed below) that you will insert into that area using the "Rules" portion of your "Write and Insert Fields" group of your Mailings Tab.

Accessing "If Then Else"

This type of statement allows you to insert different information depending upon what values your data have. In this case, we will be sending a letter to our people and will insert dates depending upon which region each customer resides in. An "*If Then Else*" statement is found in the Mailings Tab and the Rules selection in the Write & Insert Fields group

First, we need to establish the rules. Your itinerary is as follows.

Itinerary by Region	
Region	**Availability Date**
Western	**Wednesday, October 19, 2011**
Central	**Monday, October 24, 2011**
Southern	**Thursday, October 27, 2011**
Eastern	**Tuesday, November 1, 2011**
Table 3 – Itinerary	

Table 3 is a set of rules. You will be travelling to each region on these specific dates to assist your customers in the area. In order to apply these rules, you have to select the "Mailings" tab and the "rules" selection in the "Write and Insert Fields" group. Choose the *If...Then...Else* option.

Step 1: Erase the **Insert Itinerary Date** verbiage from your Master Merge Document 2. Leave the cursor in that place as you will be inserting an "*IF, then, else*" statement.

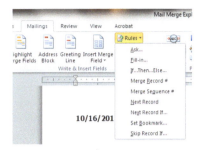

Select the "Mailings Tab" and then the "Rules" selection in the "Write and Insert Fields" group. Choose the "If....Then....Else" option.

Fig 32 – "If, Then Else" selection

After you have Selected "If Then Else", Select "Region" as shown on the left.

Fig 33 – Select "REGION" in the "Field Name"

Step 2: With the field "Region" selected in the "Field Name" drop down, write "Western" in the "compare to" box.

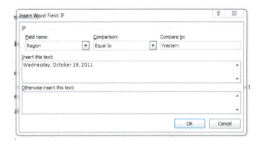

This is the first rule you are putting in. If the region is "*Western*", then put in the date: "*Wednesday, October 19, 2011*".

Fig 34 – Your First Rule – Date for Western Region

Repeat these entries until you have all four regions accounted for. Choose the dates from Table 3.

This is your second rule. If it is the "Central Region", then the date must be Monday, October 24, 2011.

Fig 35 – Your Second Rule – Date for Central Region

Complete Rules 3 and 4 for the Southern and Eastern Regions.

Having Trouble? Can't see the dates change?

In order to troubleshoot your "If Then Else" issues, right click the paragraph and select "Toggle Field Codes".

Fig 36 – Toggle Field Codes

When you enter "If Then Else" fields, you may have issues with your dates – especially in this case when you are entering multiple dates for multiple regions.

TIP 7: You can view your "If Then Else" fields by selecting the paragraph your statement is in, right clicking it and then selecting "Toggle Field Codes."

After you have chosen "Toggle Field Codes", you should see a lot of verbiage that doesn't look like English. Figure 36a shows you what your document *should* look like if you have properly inserted the "*If Then Else*" Statements. If you choose to preview your document, the dates should change, depending upon the region in the data record (A row of data). They are color coded for better visibility.

My name is John Q Public and I represent the sales division of Fluor Corporation.

I will be in your area on { IF { MERGEFIELD Region } = "Western" "Wednesday, October 19, 2011" "" } { IF { MERGEFIELD Region } = "Southern" "Thursday, October 27, 2011" "" } { IF { MERGEFIELD Region } = "Central " "Monday, October 24, 2011" "" } { IF { MERGEFIELD Region } = "Central" "Monday, October 24, 2011" "" }{ IF { MERGEFIELD Region } = "Eastern" "Tuesday, November 1, 2011" "" }. As previously stated per our phone conversation, I am in the area to check in and see how I may assist you.

Please call for confirmation as my appointments are limited on that date.

Fig 36a – Five "IF" Statements - Field Codes in a merge document

If your field codes do not look like this, you will have to re-insert the "If Then Else" Statements so that they appear as Figure 36a does.

Reinsert the "IF Then Else" fields

When you reinsert your "IF Then Else" fields, Toggle your field codes after you have entered the first date. Position the mouse pointer directly to the right of the field code Outside the field, but right next to it.

{IF { MERGEFIELD Region } = "Eastern" "Tuesday, November 1st, 2011" "" }

Position the mouse pointer directly to the right of the Bracket on the end.

Fig 36b – Positioning the Mouse pointer after the first Merge Field Statement

At that point, insert the next "If Then Else" Statement. Repeat until all five "If Then Else" statements have been inserted.

Address Block Issue Correction

TIP 8: If your address block is giving you issues, for whatever reason, insert the information individually as shown in **Figure 36**. This will give you much more control over the format.

10/17/2011

«First_Name» «Last_Name»
«Address»
«City_», «State_» «Zip»

«GreetingLine»

Address Block Issues? An alternate data entry arrangement for Using Excel Spreadsheets. Use this format if the address block gives you incorrect information.

My name is John Q Public and I repre

Fig 37 – Alternate Data Entry Format

For an example the finished product, see Appendix B - Sample Letter 2 – with date for Western Region

Step 3 – Merge your document

As with before, please select the "finish and merge" button in the Mailings Tab.

Congratulations! You now have a conditional "IF" statement in your document.

I would suggest that you practice this process and, if possible, link your learning to a real project. Do you know someone who periodically mails out flyers depending upon the region or zip code?   Are there things you want to send to one city only?   Try the "If Then Else statement on those projects.

Reference and Appendix

Reference and Credits Page

No one creates an intellectual work alone.   There are many contributors, but one writer.   Thanks to all those who had information that was useful in producing this work.

Web Sites:

1. http://www.kevinlaurence.net/essays/cc.php

2. http://www.stanford.edu/~bkunde/fb-press/articles/wdprhist.html

3. http://www.computernostalgia.net/articles/HistoryofWordProcessors.htm

4. http://www.mrmartinweb.com/type.htm

5. http://www.tekmom.com/buzzwords/zdrecord.html

Appendix A – Storing Documents

Folder Considerations

If you do not understand what a folder is on your hard drive, you need to go to http://www.jegsworks.com/ and study the concept of files and folders.

Storing files on your computer can be confusing. It is important that you have the ability to organize your files. Files on a computer can be organized much like a regular file drawer.

At work, you should adopt a strategy that puts your files and paperwork in appropriate categories and files. For example, Farmer John has his work organized by Category. At the top of the categories is **Farming Paperwork.** Within his Farming Paperwork are categories: **Apples**, **Barn Animals**, **Cherries** and **Dairy Products**.

Inside each folder would be paperwork that relates to each category. If he wanted to see Dairy paperwork, he would not look in the Apples folder.

Always try to create folders that are relevant to whatever business you work for. If you work for Farmer John and you service different divisions, create a folder for each division and put your work for each division in their respective folders.

The folder is Farming Paper work

Notice the file folders in Farming Paperwork.

They are Apples, Barn Animals, Cherries and Dairy Products.

Farmer John keeps his work organized by keeping the right paperwork in the right folder.

He would not store Dairy Product information in the Barn Animal Section and vice versa

Appendix A Figure 1 – Folder Organization Strategy

File Considerations

For more explanation of what a "file" is, check out http://www.jegsworks.com/ for a detailed lesson guide.

Ever look in a directory of a computer and wonder what it is you see? All those names!! What do they mean?   Back in the day, we used to have to have eight characters to name our files.

Can you guess what **accr1011.xls** might mean?

Let's see....the **accr** means Accounting, the **10** might mean October and the **11** might mean the year 2011. Or it might mean something else altogether different.   Today, our file names can be 255 characters long, including spacing.

Accounts Receivable Report October 2011.xls *Oohh!! It is the accounts receivable report for October of 2011.* In your work place, you should have a mindset that lends itself to others being able to tell what you are doing without having to ask you.

If you work in Payroll, maybe your file names should all start with the word Payroll.   For example, my name is Ferd Goerlitz in Payroll and I finished a report on December 21, 2011.

I could name my file: ***Payroll_FG_12212011 Report.xls***

Or I could spell it out this way:
Ferd_Goerlitz_Payroll_Report_December_21_2011.xls

This is the HR Paperwork Folder of Merge Projects

This folder is named so that it can be easily seen which file goes
 with which project.

Notice the two files have the same first name "**HR Monthly Report**"
 One is the Master and the other is the LIST

Appendix A Figure 2 – Naming your Files Appropriately

Appendix B – The OUTPUT DOCUMENTS

Sample Letter
10/27/2011

«AddressBlock»

«GreetingLine»:

I am interested in the position of administrative secretary with your company.

I have ten years experience as an executive secretary with Fluor Corporation in Irvine, California. In that position, I coordinated schedules, paying of corporate accounts, billing customers for hours and acting as liaison to the Chief Financial Officer. In my duties, I was the "go to" person for issues that revolved around company scheduling of trainings and seminars.   I was very efficient, timely and you can phone my boss at 714-555-1212 for more details.

I look forward to speaking with you soon.

Sincerely

Jane Q Public

Sample Letter 2

Insert Calendar Date

Address Block

Greeting Line

My name is John Q Public and I represent the sales division of Fluor Corporation.

I will be in your area on **Insert Itinerary Date.** As previously stated per our phone conversation, I am in the area to check in and see how I may assist you.

Please call for confirmation as my appointments are limited on that date.

Sincerely

Jane Q Sales

10/27/2011

John Jones
1234 Best St
Clovis, CA 93612

Dear John Jones,

My name is John Q Public and I represent the sales division of Fluor Corporation.

I will be in your area on **Wednesday, October 19, 2011   .** As previously stated per our phone conversation, I am in the area to check in and see how I may assist you.

Please call for confirmation as my appointments are limited on that date.

Sincerely

Jane Q Sales

www.ingramcontent.com/pod-product-compliance
Lightning Source LLC
Chambersburg PA
CBHW041145050326
40689CB00001B/496